Intermediate to Late Intermediate

THEORY FOR BUSY TEENS
BOOK 3

8 Units with Short Written Exercises to Maximize Limited Study Time

Melody Bober • Gayle Kowalchyk • E. L. Lancaster

NAME_____

 Theory for Busy Teens

is designed for students who want to develop their skills in music theory but have limited time to study it. It includes eight units devoted to the following subject areas: rhythm, augmented and diminished intervals, natural, harmonic and melodic minor scales, major and minor key signatures, musical terms and symbols, diatonic triads in major keys, five types of seventh chords, and ii-V^7-I chord progressions in major and minor keys. In addition, each book contains a mid-term review after the first four units and a final review after the last four units. The last page in the book is a comprehensive final quiz to assess knowledge in all eight areas.

Each unit includes the following:

 5-Minute FYI

A succinct introduction to the subject matter is included *for your information.*

 5-Minute Daily Workout

These short written exercises are provided for five days of the week. They contain examples that reinforce the information from the 5-Minute FYI.

 Extra Credit

This section at the end of each unit offers further challenges relating to the subject matter.

D1275492

Alfred Music Publishing Co., Inc.
P.O. Box 10003
Van Nuys, CA 91410-0003
alfred.com

ISBN-10: 0-7390-8472-0
ISBN-13: 978-0-7390-8472-4

To the Teen

To the Teacher

If you realize the importance of music theory but don't have much time to learn the subject, this book is for you. Here are some suggestions to make your study more successful.

✔ Make sure that you understand the subject matter in the 5-Minute FYI before you leave your lesson. Don't be afraid to ask your teacher questions (even if the questions seem trivial).

✔ Set aside five minutes a day to complete the daily workouts. Only complete one workout per day. It is best to do the workouts five days in a row so that you have consistent reinforcement.

✔ If you have trouble with any of the examples, go back to the 5-Minute FYI and research the answers. If you need further help, ask your teacher for assistance at the next lesson.

✔ Complete the extra credit section after you have done all of the daily workouts for the unit. Some of the extra credit sections offer further challenges so you may need help from your teacher.

✔ Avoid judging your success or knowledge of theory by comparing yourself to others. You are successful if you work consistently and gradually increase your understanding of the subject. Remember that theory can aid you with learning new music and memorizing pieces.

If you have students who realize the importance of music theory but have minimal time to learn the subject, this book is for them. Here are some suggestions to make their study more successful.

✔ Go through the 5-Minute FYI with students at the lesson. Make sure that they totally understand the theoretical concepts before leaving the lesson. Students should feel comfortable asking questions if they don't understand.

✔ When students come to a lesson without having completed the 5-Minute Daily Workouts, you may want to devote some time in the lesson to finishing them. Avoid spending the entire lesson time on this.

✔ Quickly check the students' work on the 5-Minute Daily Workouts at the lesson. Explain any incorrect answers.

✔ If students have completed the Extra Credit section, check that as well. If they have not done this section, work on it at the lesson.

✔ Help students figure out their highest priority for the next week in terms of completing theory work.

✔ Whenever possible, relate theory activities to music that the students are performing.

✔ Remember that the most successful teacher is the one who instills the love of music into every student. Theory can aid them in musical understanding.

3

Contents

Unit 1
Rhythm

Study Guide

? 5-Minute FYI

¢ = Cut Time

Cut time (or Alla Breve) is the same as $\frac{2}{2}$ time.

¢ or $\frac{2}{2}$ beats in each measure
half note gets 1 beat

Notes	Rests	Counts
o	▬	2 counts
♩.	▬ ⁊	1½ counts
♩	▬	1 count
♩.	𝄽.	¾ count
♩	𝄽	½ count
♪	⁊	¼ count

Clap and count aloud.

count: 1 - &   2   &   1 - & - 2   &   1-e-& a 2 e & a   1   &   2   &

Irregular Meter

Time signatures that do not have two beats (duple meter), three beats (triple meter), or four beats (quadruple meter) per bar are often called irregular meter.

Some frequently used irregular meters are:

$\frac{5}{4}$ beats in each measure
quarter note gets 1 beat

$\frac{5}{8}$ beats in each measure
eighth note gets 1 beat

$\frac{7}{4}$ beats in each measure
quarter note gets 1 beat

$\frac{7}{8}$ beats in each measure
eighth note gets 1 beat

Clap and count aloud.

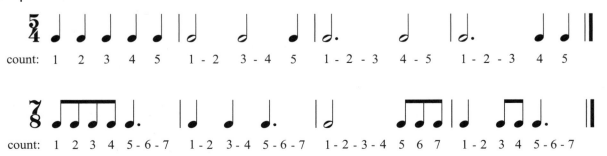

count: 1   2   3   4   5   1 - 2   3 - 4   5   1 - 2 - 3   4 - 5   1 - 2 - 3   4   5

count: 1   2   3   4   5-6-7   1-2   3-4   5-6-7   1-2-3-4   5   6   7   1 - 2   3   4   5-6-7

5

5-Minute Daily Workout No. 1

Add bar lines in the correct places in the ¢ examples. Next, write the counts below each rhythm pattern. Then clap and count aloud.

5-Minute Daily Workout No. 2

Write the counts below each ¢ rhythm pattern. Then clap and count aloud.

6

1. Write the counts below each $\frac{5}{4}$ rhythm pattern. Then clap and count aloud.

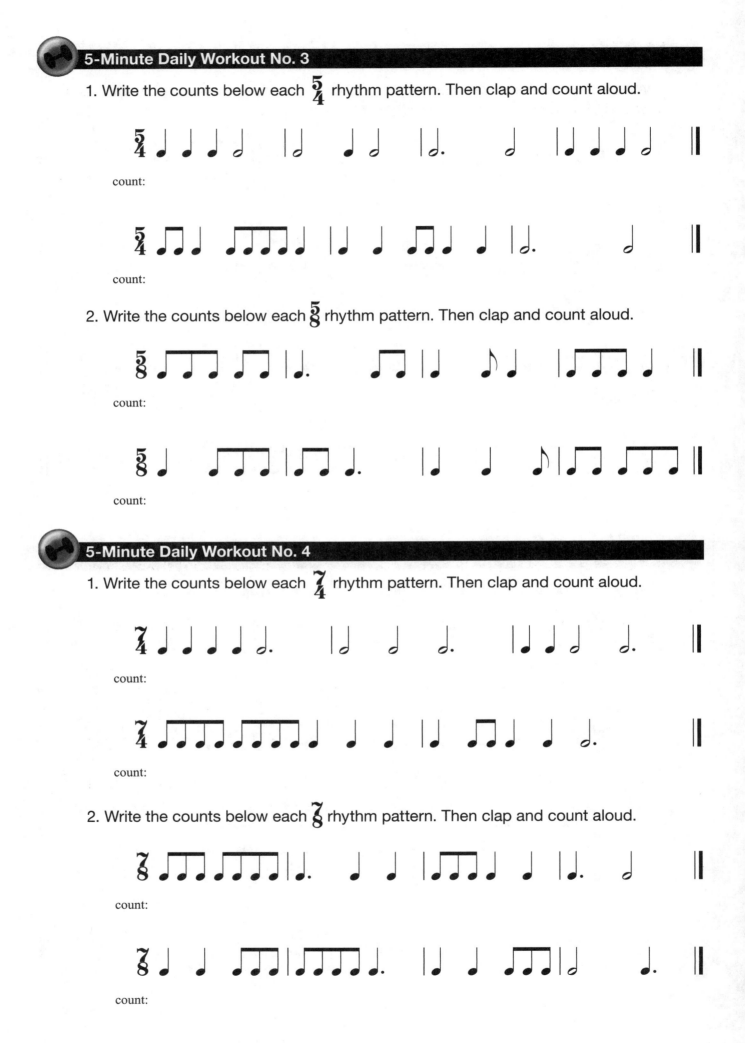

count:

count:

2. Write the counts below each $\frac{5}{8}$ rhythm pattern. Then clap and count aloud.

count:

count:

1. Write the counts below each $\frac{7}{4}$ rhythm pattern. Then clap and count aloud.

count:

count:

2. Write the counts below each $\frac{7}{8}$ rhythm pattern. Then clap and count aloud.

count:

5-Minute Daily Workout No. 5

Write the correct time signature $\frac{5}{4}$, $\frac{5}{8}$, $\frac{7}{4}$, or $\frac{7}{8}$ in the box. Next, write the counts below each rhythm pattern. Then clap and count aloud.

 Extra Credit

Mixed Meter

When two or more time signatures occur within a piece, the piece is in mixed meter.

Clap and count aloud.

count: 1 - 2   3 - 4   1   2 & 3   4   1 - 2   3   1   2 & 3   1 - 2 - 3 - 4

Write the correct time signature $\frac{4}{4}$, $\frac{3}{4}$, or $\frac{2}{4}$ in each box. Next, write the counts below each rhythm pattern. Then clap and count aloud.

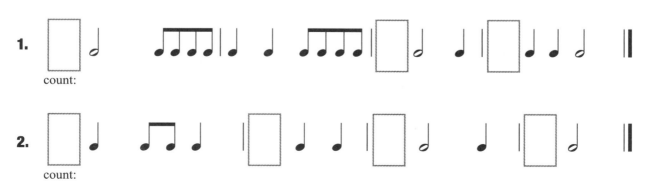

8

Unit 2
Augmented and Diminished Intervals

The intervals that occur between the keynote and each scale degree of a major scale are shown below.

Major intervals become **minor** when the distance between the two tones is *decreased* by a half step.

The word *augmented* means "made higher." Both **perfect** and **major** intervals become **augmented** (A) when the distance between the two tones is *increased* by a half step.

The word *diminished* means "made smaller." Both **perfect** and **minor** intervals become **diminished** (d) when the distance between the two tones is *decreased* by a half step.

5-Minute Daily Workout No. 1

1. Using half notes, rewrite each major 2nd or major 3rd as an augmented interval. Remember to *raise* the top note a half step to form an augmented interval.

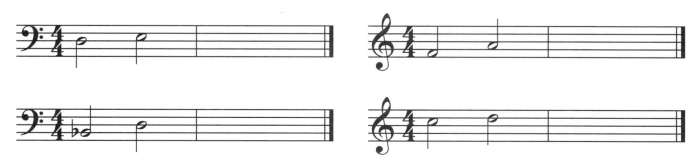

2. Using half notes, rewrite each major 2nd or major 3rd as a minor interval. Remember to *lower* the top note a half step to form a minor interval.

 5-Minute Daily Workout No. 2

1. Using half notes, rewrite each perfect 4th or perfect 5th as an augmented interval. Remember to *raise* the top note a half step to form an augmented interval.

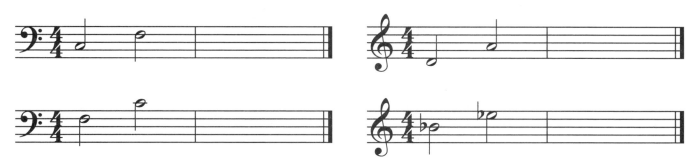

2. Using half notes, rewrite each perfect 4th or perfect 5th as a diminished interval. Remember to *lower* the top note a half step to form a diminished interval.

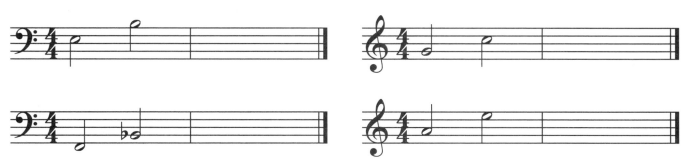

10

5-Minute Daily Workout No. 3

1. Using half notes, rewrite each major 6th or major 7th as an augmented interval. Remember to *raise* the top note a half step to form an augmented interval.

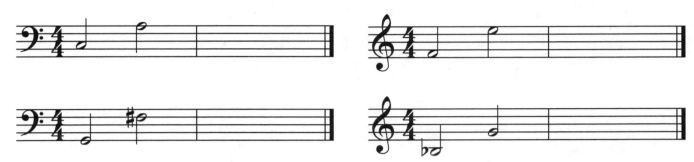

2. Using half notes, rewrite each major 6th or major 7th as a minor interval. Remember to *lower* the top note a half step to form a minor interval.

5-Minute Daily Workout No. 4

Using half notes, rewrite each minor 3rd, minor 6th, or minor 7th as a diminished interval. Remember to *lower* the top note a half step to form a diminished interval.

5-Minute Daily Workout No. 5

1. Circle A if the second interval is augmented; circle m if it is minor.

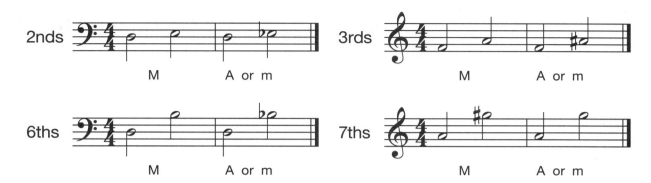

2. Circle A if the second interval is augmented; circle d if it is diminished.

 Extra Credit

1. Write the interval name on the line - m3, A3, or d3.

2. Write the interval name on the line - m6, A6, or d6.

3. Write the interval name on the line - m7, A7, or d7.

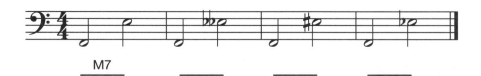

Study Guide

Unit 3
Natural, Harmonic, and Melodic Minor Scales

5-Minute FYI

Relative Minor Scales

Every major key has a **relative minor key** that has the same key signature. The relative minor begins on the 6th tone of the major scale.

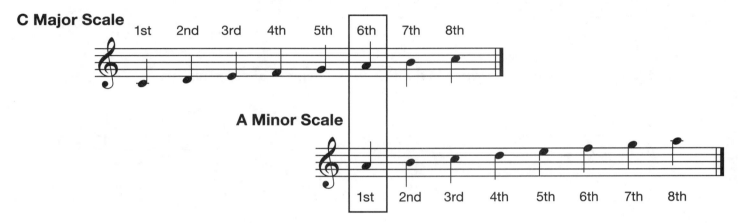

C Major Scale
1st   2nd   3rd   4th   5th   6th   7th   8th

A Minor Scale
1st   2nd   3rd   4th   5th   6th   7th   8th

The **natural minor scale** uses only the notes of the relative minor scale.

Any natural minor scale can be formed by following this sequence of whole and half steps: WHWWHWW.

The **harmonic minor scale** is the same as the natural minor scale, but with the 7th note *raised* a half step both ascending *and* descending.

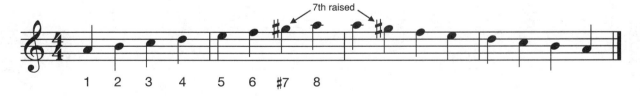
7th raised

1   2   3   4   5   6   ♯7   8

The **melodic minor scale** is the same as the natural minor scale, but with the ascending 6th and 7th notes *raised* a half step. The descending scale is the same as the natural minor.

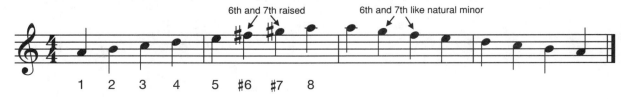
6th and 7th raised   6th and 7th like natural minor

1   2   3   4   5   ♯6   ♯7   8

5-Minute Daily Workout No. 1

1. The relative minor of C major is _____ minor.

2. Draw an accidental in front of the sixth and seventh notes of the A natural minor scale to form the ascending A melodic minor scale.

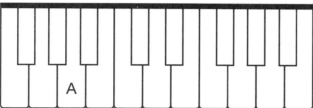

3. The sixth note of the ascending A melodic minor scale is _____ .

4. The seventh note of the ascending A melodic minor scale is _____ .

5. On the keyboard, write the letter names on the keys for the ascending A melodic minor scale.

 5-Minute Daily Workout No. 2

1. The relative minor of G major is _____ minor.

2. Draw an accidental in front of the sixth and seventh notes of the E natural minor scale to form the ascending E melodic minor scale.

3. The sixth note of the ascending E melodic minor scale is _____ .

4. The seventh note of the ascending E melodic minor scale is _____ .

5. On the keyboard, write the letter names on the keys for the ascending E melodic minor scale.

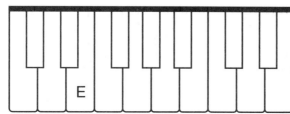

14

1. The relative minor of B-flat major is _____ minor.

2. Draw an accidental in front of the sixth and seventh notes of the G natural minor scale to form the ascending G melodic minor scale.

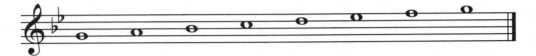

3. The sixth note of the ascending G melodic minor scale is _____ .

4. The seventh note of the ascending G melodic minor scale is _____ .

5. On the keyboard, write the letter names on the keys for the ascending G melodic minor scale.

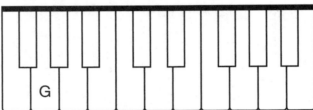

1. The relative minor of D major is _____ minor.

2. Draw an accidental in front of the sixth and seventh notes of the B natural minor scale to form the ascending B melodic minor scale.

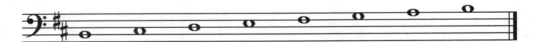

3. The sixth note of the ascending B melodic minor scale is _____ .

4. The seventh note of the ascending B melodic minor scale is _____ .

5. On the keyboard, write the letter names on the keys for the ascending B melodic minor scale.

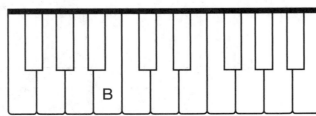

5-Minute Daily Workout No. 5

1. The relative minor of F major is _____ minor.

2. Draw an accidental in front of the sixth and seventh notes of the D natural minor scale to form the ascending D melodic minor scale.

3. The sixth note of the ascending D melodic minor scale is _____ .

4. The seventh note of the ascending D melodic minor scale is _____ .

5. On the keyboard, write the letter names on the keys for the ascending D melodic minor scale.

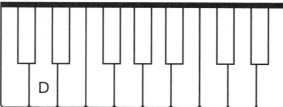

Extra Credit

Using the given fingering, play these melodic minor scales hands separately.

G Melodic Minor

B Melodic Minor

Unit 4
Major and Minor Key Signatures

 5-Minute FYI

The **key signature** indicates the notes that are to be sharped or flatted throughout the piece and aids in identifying the key in which the piece is written.

Sharps appear in the following order in the key signature:

F# C# G# D# A# E# B#

The name of a sharp major key can be determined by moving up a half step from the last sharp.

This is the key signature for the **key of B major**. A half step up from A♯ is B.

Flats appear in the following order in the key signature:

The order of flats is reversed from the order of sharps in key signatures.

B♭ E♭ A♭ D♭ G♭ C♭ F♭

The name of a flat major key can be determined by the name of the next-to-last flat.

This is the key signature for the **key of D♭ major**. The next-to-last flat is D♭.

Two major key signatures cannot be determined using the above rules:

- ✔ C Major—no sharps or flats
- ✔ F major—one flat (B♭)

Steps to Name the Minor Key from the Key Signature

1. Determine the name of the major key.

2. Go down three half steps to name the minor key.

3. Remember to skip one alphabet letter between the name of the major key and the name of the minor key.

5-Minute Daily Workout No. 1

1. Draw the sharps in the correct order on the grand staff.

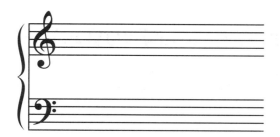

2. Circle the last sharp in each key signature. Then name the major key by going up a half step.

Key of _____ major   Key of _____ major   Key of _____ major   Key of _____ major

Key of _____ major   Key of _____ major   Key of _____ major   Key of _____ major

5-Minute Daily Workout No. 2

1. To find the name of the minor key from the key signature, go down two / three half steps from the name of the major key.

(circle one)

2. Name each minor key.

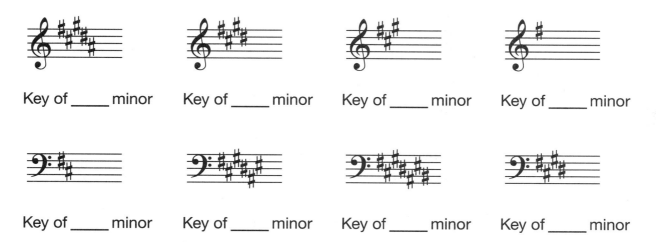

Key of _____ minor   Key of _____ minor   Key of _____ minor   Key of _____ minor

Key of _____ minor   Key of _____ minor   Key of _____ minor   Key of _____ minor

5-Minute Daily Workout No. 3

1. Draw the flats in the correct order on the grand staff.

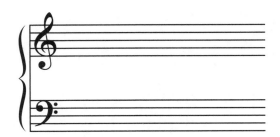

2. Circle the next-to-last flat in each key signature and name the major key.

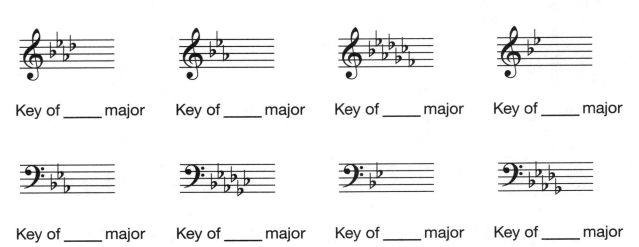

Key of _____ major   Key of _____ major   Key of _____ major   Key of _____ major

Key of _____ major   Key of _____ major   Key of _____ major   Key of _____ major

 5-Minute Daily Workout No. 4

1. The key of _____ major has one flat - B♭.

2. Name each minor key.

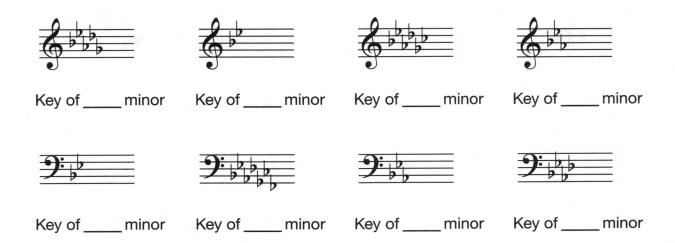

Key of _____ minor   Key of _____ minor   Key of _____ minor   Key of _____ minor

Key of _____ minor   Key of _____ minor   Key of _____ minor   Key of _____ minor

5-Minute Daily Workout No. 5

Draw a line connecting each key signature to its matching name.

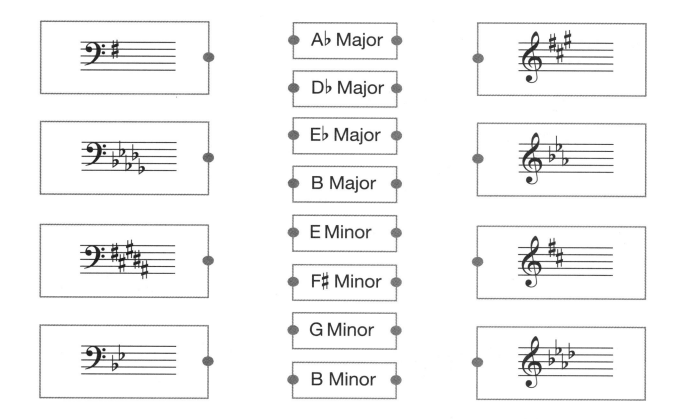

 Extra Credit

Name the major and minor key signatures in one minute to receive extra credit.

Review

 5-Minute Daily Workout No. 1

1. Add bar lines in the correct places in the example.

2. Write the interval name (M3, m3, A3, or d3) on the line.

_____   _____   _____   _____

3. Circle the incorrect note in the ascending C melodic minor scale.

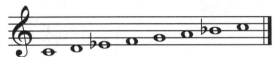

4. Name the major keys.

Key of ____ major   Key of ____ major   Key of ____ major

 5-Minute Daily Workout No. 2

1. Write the counts below the rhythm pattern. Then clap and count aloud.

count:

2. Write the interval name (P4, A4, d4, P5, A5, or d5) on the line.

_____   _____   _____   _____   _____   _____

3. Complete the ascending G melodic minor scale by writing the missing letter names.

G   A   B♭   C   D   ___   ___   G

4. Name the minor keys.

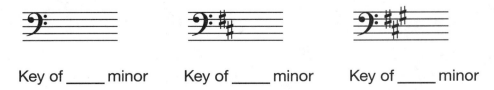

Key of ____ minor   Key of ____ minor   Key of ____ minor

5-Minute Daily Workout No. 3

1. Add bar lines in the correct places in the example.

2. Write the interval name (M6, m6, A6, or d6) on the line.

_____   _____   _____   _____

3. Draw sharps in front of the correct notes to form an ascending A melodic minor scale.

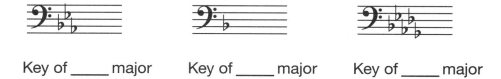

4. Name the major keys.

Key of ____ major   Key of ____ major   Key of ____ major

 5-Minute Daily Workout No. 4

1. Write the counts below the rhythm pattern. Then clap and count aloud.

count:

2. Write the interval name (M7, m7, A7, or d7) on the line.

_____   _____   _____   _____

3. Complete the ascending D melodic minor scale by drawing the missing notes.

4. Name the minor keys.

Key of ____ minor   Key of ____ minor   Key of ____ minor

Unit 5
Musical Terms and Symbols

 5-Minute FYI

The terms and symbols that follow are often found in music that you will be performing.

These terms relate to tempos.

ITALIAN	ENGLISH
Allegretto	Moderately quick tempo
Andante moderato	Moderate walking tempo
Largo	Slow, solemn
Presto	Fast, faster than allegro

These terms relate to articulation.

Accent sign (♪ ♩) — placed over or under a note that gets special emphasis; play that note louder.

Legato 𝄞 — play smoothly and connected, indicated by a curved line over or under notes.

Staccato (♪ ♩) — play short or detached, indicated by dots over or under notes.

Tenuto (♪ ♩) — hold the note for its full value.

These terms relate to dynamics.

ITALIAN	SIGN	ENGLISH
pianissimo	*pp*	very soft
piano	*p*	soft
mezzo piano	*mp*	moderately soft
mezzo forte	*mf*	moderately loud
forte	*f*	loud
fortissimo	*ff*	very loud
cresc.	<	gradually louder
decresc.	>	gradually softer

Other terms and symbols:

Dolce — sweetly

Espressivo — with expression

Molto rit. — big ritardando

Poco rit. — little ritardando

Smorzando (smorz.) — fading away

Swing style (♫ = ♪♪) — pairs of eighth notes performed in a long-short rhythm, often used in jazz-style music.

5-Minute Daily Workout No. 1

Match the Italian term on the left to its definition on the right.

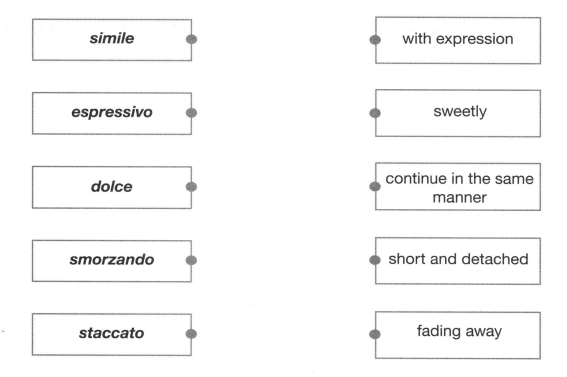

simile	with expression
espressivo	sweetly
dolce	continue in the same manner
smorzando	short and detached
staccato	fading away

5-Minute Daily Workout No. 2

1. **Tenuto** means hold the note for   half / full   value.
   (circle one)

2. **Poco rit.** means   big / little   ritardando.
   (circle one)

3. **Molto rit.** means   big / little   ritardando.
   (circle one)

4. **Largo** means   slow / fast.
   (circle one)

5. **Presto** means   slow / fast.
   (circle one)

24

Match the symbol on the left to its name on the right.

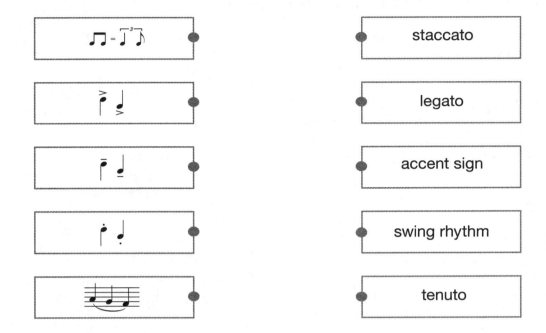

staccato

legato

accent sign

swing rhythm

tenuto

Match the symbol on the left to its definition on the right.

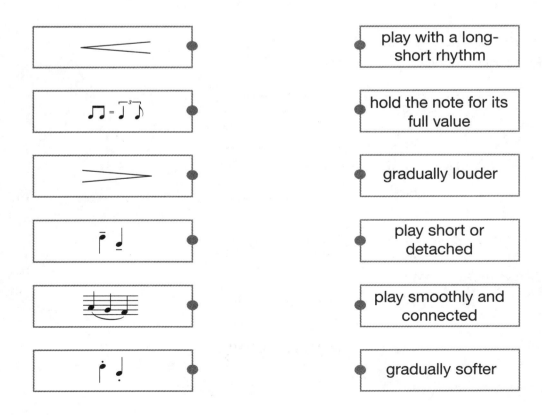

play with a long-short rhythm

hold the note for its full value

gradually louder

play short or detached

play smoothly and connected

gradually softer

25

 5-Minute Daily Workout No. 5

Write the Italian term for each symbol. Choose from the following terms:
pianissimo, piano, mezzo piano, mezzo forte, forte, fortissimo.

1. **moderately soft** _____

2. **loud** _____

3. **very soft** _____

4. **very loud** _____

5. **soft** _____

6. **moderately loud** _____

 Extra Credit

Write the definition for each term.

1. **largo** _____

2. **dolce** _____

3. **presto** _____

4. **molto rit.** _____

5. **smorzando** _____

6. **espressivo** _____

7. **poco rit.** _____

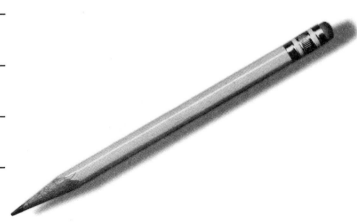

Unit 6
Diatonic Triads in Major Keys

 5-Minute FYI

✔ Triads may be built on any note of a scale.

✔ The sharps or flats in the key signature must be used when playing these triads.

✔ Triads of the key are identified by Roman numerals.

✔ These triads built on each scale degree are called **diatonic**.

Diatonic Triads in C Major are shown below.

C	Dm	Em	F	G	Am	B°	C
major	minor	minor	major	major	minor	diminished	major
I	ii	iii	IV	V	vi	vii°	I

In major keys:

    I, IV, V are major triads.

    ii, iii, vi are minor triads.

    vii° is a diminished triad.

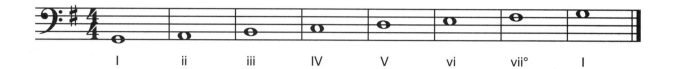

5-Minute Daily Workout No. 1

1. Using whole notes, draw a root position triad on each note of the G major scale.

    I   ii   iii   IV   V   vi   viiº   I

2. Identify the major diatonic triads in the key of G major by letter name.

I = ____ major   IV = ____ major   V = ____ major

3. Identify the minor diatonic triads in the key of G major by letter name.

ii = ____ minor   iii = ____ minor   vi = ____ minor

4. Identify the diminished diatonic triad in the key of G major by letter name.

viiº = ____ diminished

5-Minute Daily Workout No. 2

1. Using whole notes, draw a root position triad on each note of the F major scale.

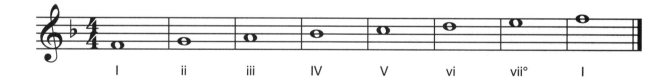

    I   ii   iii   IV   V   vi   viiº   I

2. Identify the major diatonic triads in the key of F major by letter name.

I = ____ major   IV = ____ major   V = ____ major

3. Identify the minor diatonic triads in the key of F major by letter name.

ii = ____ minor   iii = ____ minor   vi = ____ minor

4. Identify the diminished diatonic triad in the key of F major by letter name.

viiº = ____ diminished

28

1. Using whole notes, draw a root position triad on each note of the D major scale.

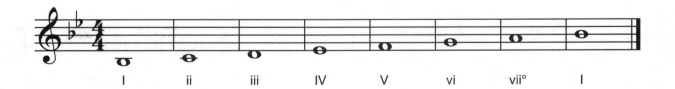

I   ii   iii   IV   V   vi   vii°   I

2. Identify the major diatonic triads in the key of D major by letter name.

I = ____ major   IV = ____ major   V = ____ major

3. Identify the minor diatonic triads in the key of D major by letter name.

ii = ____ minor   iii = ____ minor   vi = ____ minor

4. Identify the diminished diatonic triad in the key of D major by letter name.

vii° = ____ diminished

 5-Minute Daily Workout No. 4

1. Using whole notes, draw a root position triad on each note of the B♭ major scale.

I   ii   iii   IV   V   vi   vii°   I

2. Identify the major diatonic triads in the key of B♭ major by letter name.

I = ____ major   IV = ____ major   V = ____ major

3. Identify the minor diatonic triads in the key of B♭ major by letter name.

ii = ____ minor   iii = ____ minor   vi = ____ minor

4. Identify the diminished diatonic triad in the key of B♭ major by letter name.

vii° = ____ diminished

5-Minute Daily Workout No. 5

Draw a line connecting each triad to its matching Roman numeral name in the key of C major.

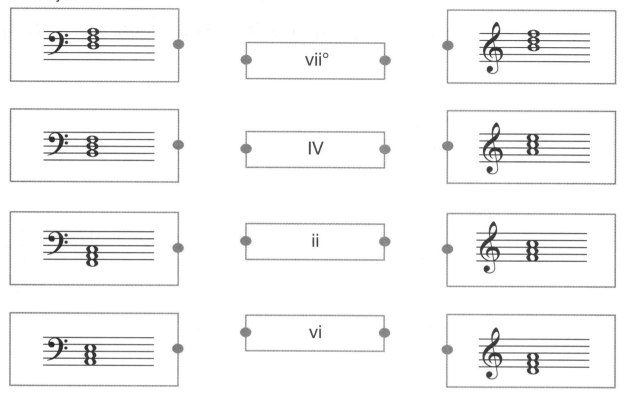

 Extra Credit

Diatonic Triads in Harmonic Minor Keys

Play the diatonic triads in A harmonic minor.

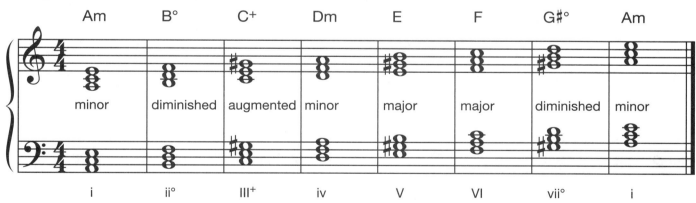

In harmonic minor keys:

i and iv are major / minor triads.
(circle one)

V and VI are major / minor triads.
(circle one)

ii° and vii° are diminished / augmented triads.
(circle one)

III⁺ is a(n) diminished / augmented triad.
(circle one)

Unit 7
Five Types of Seventh Chords

 5-Minute FYI

- There are five types of seventh chords.
- Each seventh chord consists of a triad and an interval of a seventh above the root of the triad.

Major Seventh Chord

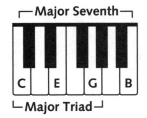

Major Triad
Major Seventh

Dominant Seventh Chord

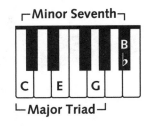

Major Triad
Minor Seventh

Minor Seventh Chord

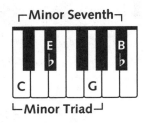

Minor Triad
Minor Seventh

Half-Diminished Seventh Chord

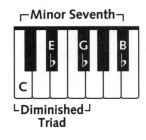

Diminished Triad
Minor Seventh

Diminished Seventh Chord

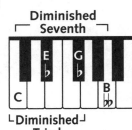

Diminished Triad
Diminished Seventh

5-Minute Daily Workout No. 1

Major Seventh Chord

A major seventh chord has 4 notes - a major triad and the interval of a major seventh above the root.

To find the major seventh, play the note a *half step* below the root of the chord and move it up an octave.

Add a major seventh to each major triad to form a major seventh chord.

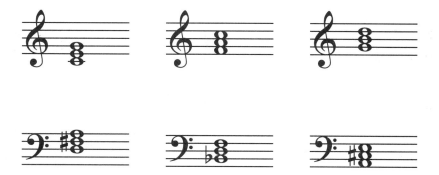

 5-Minute Daily Workout No. 2

Dominant Seventh Chord

A dominant seventh chord has 4 notes - a major triad and the interval of a minor seventh above the root.

To find the minor seventh, play the note a *whole step* below the root of the chord and move it up an octave.

Add a minor seventh to each major triad to form a dominant seventh chord.

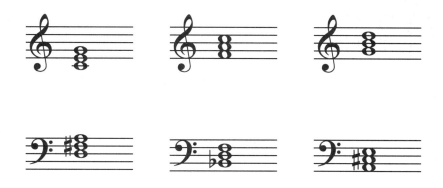

5-Minute Daily Workout No. 3

Minor Seventh Chord

A minor seventh chord has 4 notes - a minor triad and the interval of a minor seventh above the root.

To find the minor seventh, play the note a *whole step* below the root of the chord and move it up an octave.

Add a minor seventh to each minor triad to form a minor seventh chord.

 5-Minute Daily Workout No. 4

Half-Diminished Seventh Chord

A half-diminished seventh chord has 4 notes - a diminished triad and the interval of a minor seventh above the root.

To find the minor seventh, play the note a *whole step* below the root of the chord and move it up an octave.

Add a minor seventh to each diminished triad to form a half-diminished seventh chord.

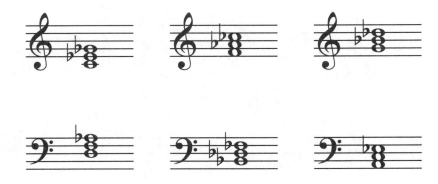

5-Minute Daily Workout No. 5

Diminished Seventh Chord

A diminished seventh chord has 4 notes - a diminished triad and the interval of a diminished seventh above the root.

To find the diminished seventh, play the note *three half steps* below the root of the chord and move it up an octave.

Add a diminished seventh to each diminished triad to form a half-diminished seventh chord.

 Extra Credit

Play the following seventh chord exercise hands separately.

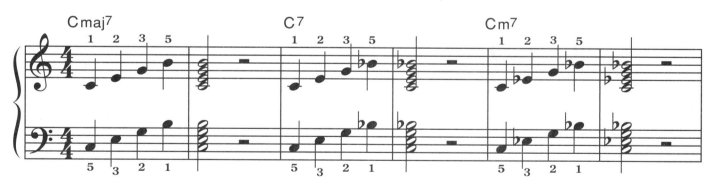

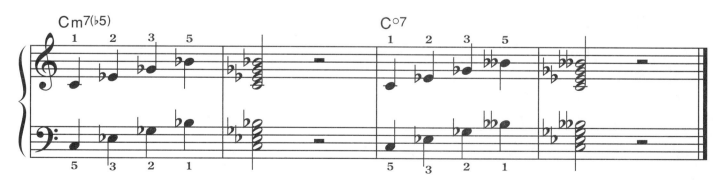

Transpose to F and G.

34

Unit 8
ii-V⁷-I Chord Progression in Major and Minor Keys

5-Minute FYI

The ii chord

In major keys, the ii chord is a minor triad.

In harmonic minor keys, the ii° chord is a diminished triad.

Key of C Major

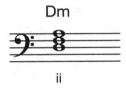

Dm

ii

Key of C Harmonic Minor

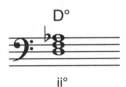

D°

ii°

The ii-V⁷-I Chord Progression

The ii-V⁷-I chord progression occurs frequently in classical, jazz, and popular music. In this progression, the **ii** chord is often played in first inversion.

Key of C Major

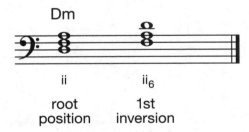

Dm

ii — root position
ii₆ — 1st inversion

Key of C Harmonic Minor

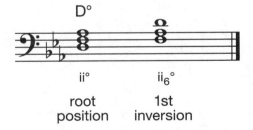

D°

ii° — root position
ii₆° — 1st inversion

Play the **ii₆-V⁷-I** chord progressions.

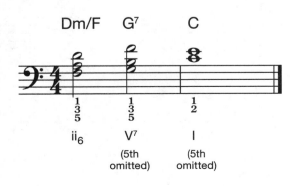

Dm/F   G⁷   C

ii₆ (5th omitted)   V⁷ (5th omitted)   I

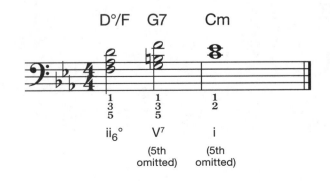

D°/F   G7   Cm

ii₆° (5th omitted)   V⁷ (5th omitted)   i

5-Minute Daily Workout No. 1

1. Using whole notes, draw a root position minor triad on scale degree 2 of the G major scale. Draw a root position dominant seventh chord on scale degree 5.

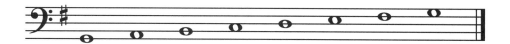

2. Play the ii_6 - V^7 - I chord progression in G major with the right hand.

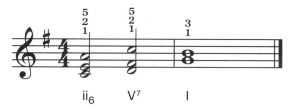

3. Play the ii_6 - V^7 - I chord progression in G major with the left hand.

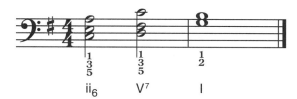

 5-Minute Daily Workout No. 2

1. Using whole notes, draw a root position diminished triad on scale degree 2 of the E harmonic minor scale. Draw a root position dominant seventh chord on scale degree 5.

2. Play the $ii_6°$ - V^7 - I chord progression in E minor with the right hand.

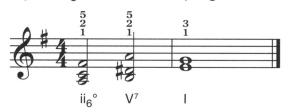

3. Play the $ii_6°$ - V^7 - I chord progression in E minor with the left hand.

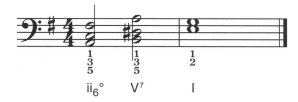

1. Using whole notes, draw a root position minor triad on scale degree 2 of the F major scale. Draw a root position dominant seventh chord on scale degree 5.

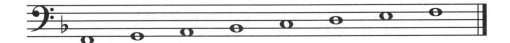

2. Play the ii_6 - V^7 - I chord progression in F major with the right hand.

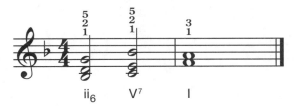

3. Play the ii_6 - V^7 - I chord progression in F major with the left hand.

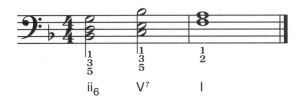

1. Using whole notes, draw a root position diminished triad on scale degree 2 of the D harmonic minor scale. Draw a root position dominant seventh chord on scale degree 5.

2. Play the $ii_6°$ - V^7 - I chord progression in D minor with the right hand.

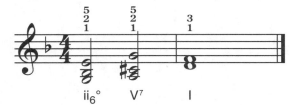

3. Play the $ii_6°$ - V^7 - I chord progression in D minor with the left hand.

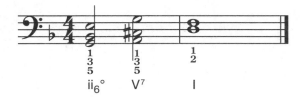

5-Minute Daily Workout No. 5

1. Using whole notes, draw a root position minor triad on scale degree 2 of
   the D major scale. Draw a root position dominant seventh chord on scale degree 5.

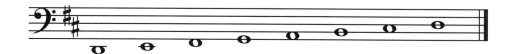

2. Play the ii₆ - V⁷ - I chord progression in D major with the right hand.

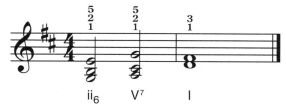

3. Play the ii₆ - V⁷ - I chord progression in D major with the left hand.

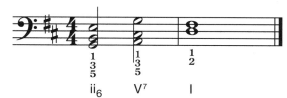

★ Extra Credit

Play the I - ii₆ - V⁷ - I chord progression in B-flat major with the left hand.

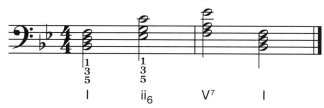

Play the melody of *Hanukkah* with the RH adding the chords that are shown below the
staff with the LH. Use the chord inversions shown above.

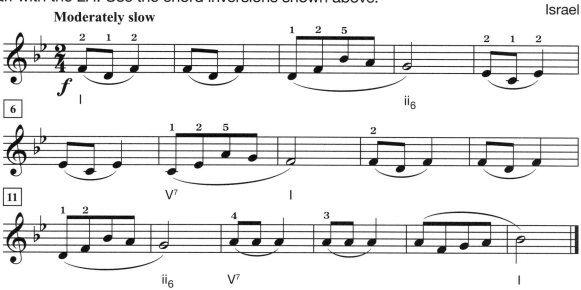

Review

Final Review

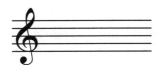 **5-Minute Daily Workout No. 1**

getting bigger
1. *Smorzando* means fading away.
(circle one)

2. Using whole notes, draw a root position IV chord in C major.

3. This is a major / dominant seventh chord.
(circle one)

4. Play the ii₆° - V⁷ - I chord progression in E minor.

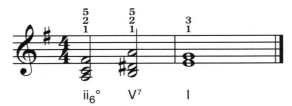

ii₆°   V⁷   I

 **5-Minute Daily Workout No. 2**

sweetly
1. *Dolce* means boldly.
(circle one)

2. Using whole notes, draw a root position ii chord in G major.

3. This is a dominant / minor seventh chord.
(circle one)

4. Play the ii₆ - V⁷ - i chord progression in G major.

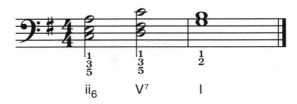

ii₆   V⁷   I

5-Minute Daily Workout No. 3

1. ***Presto*** means <u>slow</u> <u>fast</u> .
(circle one)

2. Using whole notes, draw a root position V chord in F major.

3. This is a <u>diminished</u> <u>half-diminished</u> seventh chord.
(circle one)

4. Play the ii₆ - V⁷ - I chord progression in F major.

ii₆   V⁷   I

5-Minute Daily Workout No. 4

1. ***Largo*** means <u>slow</u> <u>fast</u> .
(circle one)

2. Using whole notes, draw a root position iii chord in C major.

3. This is a <u>major</u> <u>minor</u> seventh chord.
(circle one)

4. Play the ii₆° - V⁷ - i chord progression in D minor.

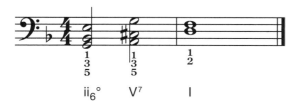

ii₆°   V⁷   i

Quiz

Extra Credit

1. Write the counts below the rhythm pattern. Then clap and count aloud.

count:

2. Circle the name of each interval.

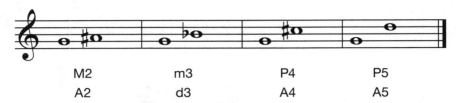

M2	m3	P4	P5
A2	d3	A4	A5

3. Circle the incorrect note in the ascending D melodic minor scale.

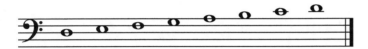

4. Name each major key and its relative minor.

Key of ____ major   Key of ____ major   Key of ____ major   Key of ____ major

____ minor   ____ minor   ____ minor   ____ minor

5. ***Allegretto*** means a moderately slow / moderately fast tempo.
(circle one)

6. Using whole notes, draw the root position triads in C major.

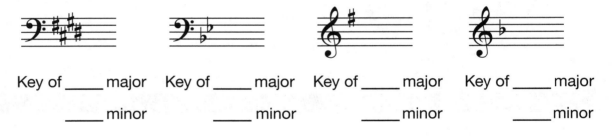

iii   V

7. This is a dominant / major seventh chord.
(circle one)

8. Play the ii₆ - V⁷ - i chord progression in D major.

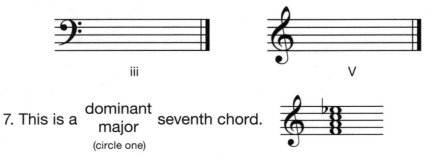

ii₆   V⁷   I

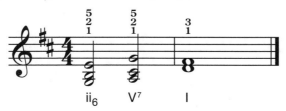